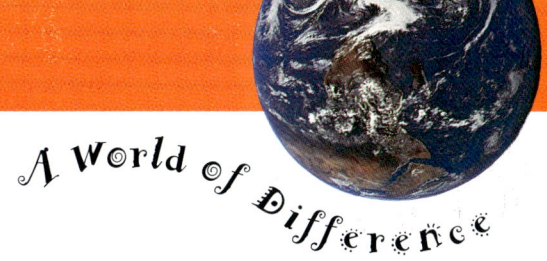
A World of Difference

Animals and Us

By Sara Corbett

CHILDRENS PRESS®
CHICAGO

Picture Acknowledgments
Cover (top left), NASA; cover (left), © Victor Englebert; cover (top right), © Richard T. Nowitz/Photri; cover (bottom right), © Barry W. Barker/Odyssey/Chicago; 1, © R. Harding/Photri; 3 (left), © Keren Su/Tony Stone Images; 3 (top right), © Reinhard Brucker; 3 (bottom right), © David R. Frazier/Tony Stone Images; 4 (left), © Penny Tweedie/Tony Stone Images; 4 (center right), © Walt Anderson/Visuals Unlimited; 4 (bottom right), © Reinhard Brucker; 5 (left), © Leonard Lee Rue/SuperStock International, Inc.; 5 (top right), © Jean-Marie Jro/Valan; 5 (bottom right), © David Hiser/Tony Stone Images; 6 (left), © R. Harding/Photri; 6 (right), © Jane P. Downton/Root Resources; 7 (top), © Science VU/Visuals Unlimited; 7 (bottom), © F. Lerner/SuperStock International Inc.; 8 (left), © SuperStock International, Inc.; 8 (right), © E. Carle/SuperStock International Inc.; 9 (left) and 9 (top right), © Robert Frerck/Odyssey/Chicago; 9 (bottom right), © Chip and Rosa Maria de la Cueva Peterson; 10 (left), © Michael Elvan Habicht/Photri; 10 (right), © Buddy Mays/Travel Stock; 11 (top left), © William J. Weber/Visuals Unlimited; 11 (top right), © N. Pecnik/Visuals Unlimited; 11 (bottom), © Rob & Melissa Simpson/Valan; 12 (left), Jeannie R. Kemp/Valan; 12 (right), © Michael Dick/Animals Animals; 13 (left), © David L. Pearson/Visuals Unlimited; 13 (top right), © Carl Purcell; 13 (bottom right), The Bettmann Archive; 14 (left), © Christine Osborne/Valan; 14 (right), © Robert Frerck/Odyssey/Chicago; 15 (top), © Paul Chesley/Tony Stone Images; 15 (bottom left), © Jean Sloman/Valan; 15 (bottom right) © Reinhard Brucker; 16 (left), The Bettmann Archive; 16 (right), © North Wind Pictures; 17 (left), © Robert Frerck/Odyssey/Chicago; 17 (top right), Stock Montage; 17 (bottom right), UPI/Bettmann Newsphotos; 18 (left), © Victor Englebert; 18 (right), © Nicholas DeVore/Tony Stone Images; 19 (top), © SuperStock International, Inc., 19 (center), © Paul Chesley/Tony Stone Images; 19 (bottom), © SuperStock International, Inc.; 20 (left), © Wolfgang Kaehler; 20 (top right), © Field Museum, Chicago/Reinhard Brucker; 20 (bottom right), © Paul Chesley/Tony Stone Images; 21 (top left), © Barry Lewis/Tony Stone Images; 21 (center), © Charles Preitner/Visuals Unlimited; 21 (top right), © Zefa-U.K./H.Armstrong Roberts; 21 (bottom right), © Michael Scott/Tony Stone Images; 22 (top), © Cameramann International, Ltd.; 22 (bottom), The Bettmann Archive; 23 (top), © Jeff Greenberg/Unicorn Stock Photos; 23 (bottom), © Carl Purcell; 23 (right), © Alan Briere/SuperStock International, Inc.; 24 (left), © Richard T. Nowitz/Photri; 24 (right), © Robert Frerck/Odyssey/Chicago; 25 (top), © Chip and Rosa Maria de la Cueva Peterson; 25 (bottom left), © Paul Harris/Tony Stone Images; 25 (bottom right), © Carl Purcell; 26 (left), The Bettmann Archive; 26 (top right), © Christine Osborne/Valan; 26 (bottom right), © Jim Shippee/Unicorn Stock Photos; 27 (left), © Ian Murphy/Tony Stone Images; 27 (right), © David Frazier/Tony Stone Images; 28 (left), © Mauritius/SuperStock International, Inc.; 28 (top right), © SuperStock International, Inc.; 28 (bottom right), © Robert Frerck/Odyssey/Chicago; 29 (top), © Porterfield/Chickering; 29 (bottom), © Gary Brettnacher/SuperStock International, Inc.; 30 (top), © Alan Briere/SuperStock International, Inc.; 30 (bottom), © Leonardo Editrice/SuperStock International, Inc.; 31 (top), © Leonard Lee Rue/SuperStock International, Inc.; 31 (center), © Mary & Lloyd McCarthy/Root Resources; 31 (bottom), UPI/Bettmann

On the cover
Left: Tuareg girl carrying lambs, Niger
Top: Camel rider, Egypt
Bottom: Children with pet birds, Panama

On the title page
Bronze horse-and-carriage sculpture, China, c. 100 A.D.

Project Editor Shari Joffe
Design Herman Adler Design Group
Photo Research Feldman & Associates

Library of Congress Cataloging-in-Publication Data

Corbett, Sara.
    Animals and us / by Sara Corbett.
       p. cm. — (A world of difference)
    ISBN 0-516-08177-2
    1. Human–animal relationships—Juvenile literature. 2. Animals—Juvenile literature. [1. Human–animal relationships. 2. Animals.]
.I. Title. II. Series.
QL85.C67   1995
591–dc20
                                                        95-7024
                                                          CIP
                                                           AC

Copyright 1995 by Childrens Press®, Inc.
All rights reserved. Published simultaneously in Canada.
Printed in the United States of America.
1 2 3 4 5 6 7 8 9 10 R 04 03 02 01 00 99 98 97 96 95

Contents

Animals All Around Us **4**

Animals Make Good Friends. **8**

Animals and Power **12**

Animals and Beliefs. **14**

Animals Help Us to Survive **18**

Hoofing Around **24**

Sharing the Work. **26**

Animals and Entertainment **28**

Endangered Animals. **30**

Animals All Around Us

Nearly everybody has a favorite animal. What's yours? Maybe you like to go see the giraffes at the zoo. Perhaps there's a rabbit that lives in your backyard, or you've seen pictures of beautiful animals that come from faraway places. Maybe your favorite animal is a dog or cat or another kind of pet that lives right in your house!

Have you ever thought about what makes animals so special? We might think of animals as cute or fun to play with, but the relationship between humans and animals has a long and interesting history, one that goes far beyond having pets.

Aborigine child with young kangaroo, Australia

Animal stamps from Madagascar and Poland
Many countries celebrate their native animals by designing postage stamps in their honor.

Polar bear at the zoo, Singapore
The zoo is a great place to see animals from other parts of the world.

Hippopotami, Zimbabwe Animals are most interesting when they're in their natural habitats. Because animals don't like to be disturbed in the wild, the best way to see them is through binoculars—or, if they're across the globe, in photographs!

Tarahumara Indian woman with lambs, Mexico

Artifacts from prehistoric times depict animals as playing a central role in people's lives. Centuries later, as early explorers made their way to remote parts of the world, they often relied on animals to guide them. In the 1300s, explorers from the island of Tahiti got into their canoes and followed migrating birds across the ocean, where they discovered the islands of Hawaii.

Animals also have special instincts and abilities that people don't have. We admire animals for their beauty, strength, speed, and ability to survive in conditions that we can't. Sometimes we even look to animals to see what the weather's going to be.

Chinese bronze sculpture, c. 100 A.D.

One day in 1974, in the Lianoning province of China, people noticed animals acting strangely. Geese were flying in circles, pigs bit off one another's tails, and rats started running down the streets in packs. Several days later, a huge earthquake hit the area, but nearly everyone escaped. Why? Because they realized that the animals were sensing a natural disaster and they evacuated the area!

Assyrian horse and chariot
Ancient wall carvings, sculptures, and paintings from many parts of the world show that animals have helped humans for thousands of years. The Assyrians, who lived in the northern part of present-day Iraq, ruled an empire that lasted from about 1500 B.C. to 600 B.C.

Cave drawings, Algeria
These drawings were made over 8,000 years ago. They show that prehistoric people hunted animals like wild horses and bulls, probably for food and clothing.

Painting of elephant and rider, India, 1500s

Around the world, and throughout time, animals have been and continue to be an important part of people's lives. How are animals a part of your life?

7

Animals Make Good Friends

Do you have a pet? If you do, you probably think of your pet as one of your best friends. Pets can be important members of a family, needing the same love, care, and respect that people do. In parts of Europe, people can bring their dogs to restaurants with them. Some restaurants even have special pet menus, so you can order your dog a meal to eat right at the table with you!

People have had pets since prehistoric days. About 15,000 years ago, the first dogs were tamed to live in hunting villages. The cat has been a popular pet since the days of ancient Egypt, when cats were so sacred that if one died, it was mummified and buried in a special cat cemetery.

Today, if you visit a pet shop or animal breeder in your neighborhood, you're likely to see animals that originally came from different parts of the world. The iguana, the cockatoo, and the guinea pig, for example, are animals native to South America that are kept as pets all over the world.

Dog mosaic, ancient Rome During the first century, A.D., Romans who had dogs were required to keep a mosaic picture like this one with the words *"Cave canem"* ("Beware the dog") outside the entrance to their homes.

Ancient Egyptian statue Cats were first domesticated as pets by the ancient Egyptians in the 16th century B.C. Cats were considered sacred because the Egyptians believed that the spirit of an important deity sometimes resided in them.

Armadillos, Mexico Often, people domesticate animals that live in the surrounding environment. Armadillos, which live in dry, desert regions, are kept as pets in parts of Mexico and other Latin American countries.

Boys with pet bird, Morocco

Girl with pet lamb, Argentina

We now know enough about these different kinds of animals and how they breed that we can provide them with the right temperature, food, and setting to live comfortably, even in a place that's thousands of miles away from their native land. Unfortunately, some exotic animals, like tropical birds and monkeys, are captured and sold illegally as pets.

In certain parts of the world, you'll find people with pets from the surrounding environment. These types of pets can give you clues to their natural habitat. For example, in the warm, forested regions of Madagascar, the tree-dwelling chameleon is a popular pet. In Alaska and northern Canada, big furry dogs like the Malamute are good pets because they can withstand very cold temperatures.

Boy with pet three-toed sloth, Brazil The three-toed sloth is a mammal native to the tropical rain forests of South America.

Kids with pet monitor, United States These kids are holding a water monitor, a type of lizard native to parts of Asia and Australia.

Chameleon, Madagascar
This curious little reptile is famous for changing colors, from green to brown, depending on the temperature of the air.

Samoyed, Canada The powerful, furry Samoyed was originally bred to herd reindeer and caribou in frosty Siberia, but today Samoyeds are just as comfortable being family dogs.

Tarantula These hairy spiders are commonly found in the southwestern United States and are thought to be dangerous. But people who have tarantulas for pets can assure you that their bite is no worse than a bee sting.

Animals and Power

For centuries, animals have been a symbol of power and wealth in many cultures. In herding societies, the greater number of animals people have in their flocks, the wealthier they are. For instance, among the Sami people, who live in far northern Europe above the arctic circle, a family's social status depends on the number of reindeer it possesses.

Certain animals also have been favored by rulers. In the late 1700s, King Louis XVI of France carried a falcon on his left wrist as a symbol of his nobility. During the 11th century, the king of Norway was removed from office for being a poor ruler. When he was returned to power, he was so angry at his subjects for deposing him that he crowned his dog, Saur, king. The dog held the crown for three full years!

Coat of arms, Canada A coat of arms signifies the history, values, and talents of a family. Regal animals such as lions and eagles are often included in a coat of arms.

Quetzal, Guatemala The vividly colored quetzal was treasured by the Aztec emperors, who kept collections of the birds in immense cages. Only an emperor was allowed to wear the plumes of the quetzal. Anyone else caught wearing them was put to death. Today, the quetzal is the national emblem of Guatemala.

Masai cattle herders, Kenya
The Masai people of Kenya and Tanzania live mainly by herding cattle. Like the Quechua people, the social status of Masai families is measured by how many animals they have in their herd.

Llama herds, Peru The Quechua people live in the Andes mountains of Ecuador, Peru, and Bolivia. Many Quechua make their living herding llamas. The more llamas a family has in its herd, the more prominence it has in the community.

Falcon, United Arab Emirates
Falcons are popular pets among wealthy members of Arab culture. They are good hunters and loyal companions.

13

Animals and Beliefs

Because there's so much we don't know about the way animals live, interact and think, they are full of mystery for humans. In fact, animals play a significant role in the spiritual beliefs of many cultures. The Quechua people of South America believe that animals have come to them as a "loan" from God, so they're careful to treat the animals very kindly. The Assumbo people of Nigeria consider the colobus monkeys that live in the nearby forest to be prophets.

Cow, India In some parts of India, cows are allowed to roam free in the streets. This is because most Hindus revere the cow as a sacred animal.

In India, the Hindu faith holds all cows to be sacred, making cows the most cared-for creatures in that country. Still other animals are feared in some cultures. The cat, which was a sacred animal in ancient Egypt, was feared as a carrier of black magic in Europe during the Middle Ages. In those days, cats were hunted and tortured in the name of warding off evil. Yet, as the cat population decreased, the number of disease-carrying rats grew, and by the 17th century, people seemed to realize that cats were, in fact, good animals to have around.

Witch and black cat, England Fear and superstition involving cats go back to the Middle Ages in Europe, when people were regularly accused of being witches and practicing black magic.

Bear kachina doll The Hopi people of the southwestern United States believe in powerful ancestral spirits called *kachinas*. They sometimes make dolls of the *kachinas*. One of the *kachinas* takes the form of the bear. Among the Hopi, the bear is believed to be so strong that it can cure the sick.

Japanese priests leading ceremony to honor puffer fish In Japan, the puffer fish, or *fugu,* is both respected and feared. Though it is considered to be the most delicious of all fishes, it can be deadly if not prepared by a specially trained *fugu* chef who knows how to remove a poisonous gland inside the fish.

Colobus monkey, Nigeria Colobus monkeys populate the deep forest of Nigeria, near where the Assumbo people live. Assumbo legend says that it was these monkeys who informed the people that there was only one god. For this reason, the monkeys are believed to be spiritual messengers.

The mystery surrounding animals has led to a number of beliefs about the existence of mythical creatures. For instance, in roughly 2300 B.C., when ancient Greek traders saw men from Mesopotamia (now Iraq) riding horses for the first time, they believed them to be strange animals, half man and half horse. These "animals" were called centaurs and became a central part of many Greek legends. The mermaid is another fantastical creature, half woman and half fish, about whom many stories have been told.

Gryphon, India With the head and wings of an eagle, the body of a lion, and the tail of the serpent, this strange beast, believed to guard the great treasures of India, was certainly something to be feared!

Unicorn from a 16th-century Swiss book This magical creature serves as a symbol of purity and elegance. It was widely believed that the unicorn's single horn contained a special fluid that could cure any sickness.

Mermaid, England Hundreds of years ago, mermaids were greatly feared by European sailors, who viewed them as creatures sent from the underworld to tempt them into the deadly waters of the sea. But on occasion, sailors told stories of beautiful mermaids actually rescuing them from drowning. Belief in mermaids may have been influenced by the strange cries that many sailors reported hearing while at sea. Today, experts theorize that what the sailors really were hearing were whale songs!

Dragon sculpture, Hong Kong Dragons were believed to have wings and breathe fire on all who opposed them. Generally seen as evil creatures, dragons became a part of many traditional stories in Asia and other areas of the world.

Centaur, ancient Greece The centaur was thought to be half man and half horse and was famous in Greek legends for drinking a lot of wine and running away with helpless maidens.

Animals Help Us to Survive

Since prehistoric times, people have relied on animals to provide food, shelter, and clothing to keep them alive. In fact, without the help of animals, it's doubtful that the human species would ever have survived. To this day, we still depend on animals for these things, but some people question whether we really need to depend on animals as much as we have in the past.

The issue of how we treat animals is an important one in today's world. Animal rights groups have organized protests against hunting, whaling, wearing fur, and using animals for laboratory tests. Other people argue that animal hunting is an important part of various cultural practices or is still key to the survival of people in some areas of the world. Especially in places where there's not

Spear fishers, Cook Islands People who live by the sea, such as those who live on the islands of the South Pacific, tend to have diets that rely heavily on seafood.

Samburu girl milking goat, Kenya In most parts of the world, cows or goats provide an important part of people's diets: milk! Milk is also used to make other dairy products, like butter and cheese. In some areas, other animals, including llamas and camels, provide healthy dairy products as well.

Beef cattle, United States The United States is the world's largest producer of beef. Americans eat more beef than any other kind of meat.

Farmer herding geese, Indonesia Geese, turkeys, chickens, and other kinds of fowl—as well as their eggs—are eaten in many cultures around the world.

a grocery store on every corner, certain cultures still need animals to help them stay nourished, warm, and protected.

Many cultures are shaped by the availability of certain animals as food. For instance, in Iceland, where the climate makes it nearly impossible to grow vegetables or foster animal life, the seaside culture revolves around fishing for herring and cod. In nomadic cultures of Asia and Africa, people can survive long periods of time in the desert by eating the cheese-like milk of the camel.

Witchity grubs, Australia Protein, which helps build strong bones, is a necessary part of the human diet. In some dry desert areas where there are few animals, such as parts of Africa and Australia, insect larvae are the most available sources of protein.

Nearly everyone owns at least one piece of clothing that comes from an animal. Wool, which is made from the thick coats, or "fleece," of animals like sheep, goats, llama, and alpaca, is one of the world's most common fabrics. In the arctic, people wear outfits made of seal skin and caribou fur to keep them warm and dry in cold and snowy weather.

Inuit caribou-fur parka
The Inuit people live in the arctic regions of North America and in Greenland. Many Inuit people don't have stores to shop at, so they must rely on the few arctic animals—namely seal, caribou, and polar bears—to supply them with clothing. Because these animals are naturally suited for the cold climate, their skins and furs provide lots of warmth and protection from wind, water, and snow.

Silk merchant, China (above) **and silk farm, Japan** (right)
Did you know that silk comes from a special kind of caterpillar? Silk clothing is expensive because workers must unwind the cocoons of the silkworm by hand before the threads can be used to weave garments. Silk was discovered in China sometime around 2700 B.C. The process of making silk was kept secret by the Chinese for 3000 years.

Leather shoes Cow leather, available in many countries throughout the world, is one of the most common materials used to make shoes.

Man shearing sheep, New Zealand A sheep isn't hurt by having its wool sheared—it's just like getting a haircut! People in nearly every part of the world raise sheep for clothing or food. In New Zealand, a major sheep-producing country, there are about 20 sheep for every person!

Wool robe, Yemen You would think that the nomadic people of the Middle East wear robes made from a lightweight fabric like cotton, but they don't. The robes are white and loose-fitting to reflect the sun and circulate air, but they're made from wool to keep their wearers warm at night, when the desert can actually get quite cold.

Alpaca, Peru The thick wool of the alpaca, a close relative of the llama, is often dyed colorful colors and knitted into bulky, warm shirts and sweaters that are sold all over North and South America.

Animals have helped to provide people around the world with shelter. The Bedouin people of the Middle East use camel hair to make tents that are sturdy and will protect them from the wind and sand of the desert. In the southern part of Africa, people use the clay mud from large anthills to make bricks for houses and farm buildings.

Bedouin tents, Jordan These camel-hair tents can hold up in the nastiest of sandstorms, and yet they're lightweight enough that they can be easily packed up and carried to another location.

Wall, India Though the circles on this wall look decorative, they actually serve an important purpose. They are made of cow manure that has been patted into cakes. After they dry on the wall, they will be used as fuel to build a fire for cooking and warmth.

Masai house, Tanzania
The Masai people depend on their cattle herds not only for food, but also for shelter—their homes are made of branches plastered over with cattle dung. The dung dries to a hard, waterproof covering that helps keep away termites.

Athabascan animal-skin hut, Alaska In the past, many Native American peoples, including the Athabascans of the Northwest, made shelters out of poles covered with animal skins.

Yurt, Kazakhstan The Kazakh people live mainly in Kazakhstan and China. Many Kazakhs are nomadic herders of sheep, horses, goats, and cattle. They live in warm, portable, round huts called *yurts*. The traditional *yurt* has a frame of wood over which is stretched a cover of felt made from pressed animal hair.

Hoofing Around

Before we had cars, trains, and planes, we had animals to help us get from here to there. Even today, there are certain areas where traveling by animal is the most effective way to go. In Malaysia, where much of the land is swampy, people ride water buffaloes, which are strong animals that can easily make it through the densest swamp. In Alaska and northern Canada, where deep snow often buries the roads, one of the best ways to get around is by dogsled. The dogs—huskies, malamutes, or samoyeds—are specially bred to thrive in cold weather.

We rely on animals to transport our belongings as well. Without "pack animals" like horses, mules, yaks, and oxen, our civilization would have advanced at a much slower rate than it has.

Camel, Egypt Famous for its ability to walk for days without getting tired or needing water, the camel has been called the "ship of the desert." It remains a popular means of travel in the desert regions of the Middle East.

Yak, Nepal In Nepal, where the Himalaya mountains rise to over 25,000 feet, the yak is a dependable mode of transportation. Its sturdy legs allow it to climb steep and rocky mountain passes, while its bulk makes it great for carrying heavy loads and even people up to 20 miles in a day.

Horses, Paraguay The horse is one of the most important animals used in human transportation. Throughout history, when food became scarce in one area, horses helped people to pick up and move themselves to a new place.

Elephant, Thailand The elephant is a good means of transportation because it is intelligent, strong, and dependable.

Reindeer sled, Siberia In arctic regions, where deep snow covers the ground much of the year, one of the best ways to get around is on a sled pulled by either dogs or reindeer.

25

Sharing the Work

Animals sometimes make the work we do a lot easier. From dogs that are skilled at herding cattle to tiny capuchin monkeys that accomplish small tasks for people with disabilities, animals are about the greatest helpers you can imagine!

Carrier pigeon The carrier pigeon can fly long distances at 30 miles per hour, making it a useful messenger. During the Franco-Prussian war (1870-71), carrier pigeons flew numerous important political messages to members of the French army who had crossed enemy lines. Today, there's a memorial in Paris dedicated to the war-hero pigeons.

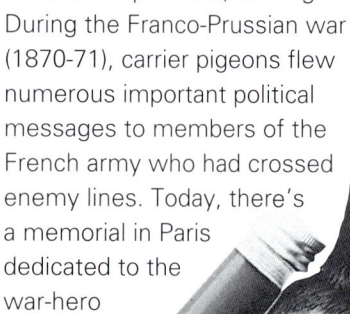

Monkey learning to pick coconuts, Thailand
Climbing tall trees to pick fruit or nuts is difficult for humans, but easy for monkeys! So in Thailand, monkeys are taught to climb palm trees and then spin coconuts until they break off from the branch and fall to the ground.

Border collie, Scotland Herding dogs are important assistants to shepherds around the world. Originally bred along the border of Scotland and England, border collies guard sheep that roam freely over field and meadow.

Oxen pulling cart of vegetables, Zimbabwe
Oxen, which are strong enough to pull plows and other heavy loads, are used as work animals in countries all over the world.

Guide dog A guide dog goes through several years of training before it becomes a companion to someone who is visually impaired. Most often these dogs come from the most trustworthy and intelligent dog breeds.

Animals and Entertainment

If you have a pet, you probably know that animals can be lots of fun. In fact, several forms of entertainment have sprung from the idea that animals are exciting to watch. Sadly, in many instances, people have used animals to please a crowd without much regard for their health or happiness. This is something that is slowly beginning to change, at least in some parts of the world, as we gain a greater understanding about animals and their needs.

For instance, the traditional circus, which once featured elephants that could stand on their heads, bears riding bicycles, and lions and tigers jumping through hoops, has in many places been replaced by performances that emphasize human tricks and acrobatics. New rules and

Circus, Canada Circuses around the world have traditionally featured animals performing feats designed to entertain large audiences. Circuses existed as far back as ancient Rome, where emperors enjoyed matching elephants, rhinos, bears, and lions against one another in well-attended, bloody fights.

Polo, England Polo, a game in which players on horseback use mallets to hit a ball through goalposts, is a popular sport in England.

Cockfighting, Indonesia Cockfighting is a spectator sport in which trained roosters fight one another until one or both of the animals dies.

Bullfight, Portugal This type of competition takes place in Portugal, Spain, southern France, and Latin America. Usually, the matador, or bullfighter, is expected to dodge the charges of an angry bull with the ultimate goal of killing it. In Portuguese bullfighting, however, the bull is never killed.

regulations in many countries work to ensure that animals working in entertainment are properly cared for.

Animals are also a part of several sports, including polo and horseracing, that are popular all over the world.

Rodeo riding, United States The rodeo offers a lot of excitement to participants and spectators alike. One event is a contest in which riders compete to stay on a bucking steer for the longest amount of time.

Endangered Animals

In nearly every place in the world, species of animals that once thrived have now become extinct. Extinction, which means the very last member of a species dies out, is caused by everything from hunting, to illegal pet trading, to the destruction of ecosystems that are home to many animals.

Endangered animals are those whose numbers have dropped so low that they are in danger of becoming extinct. All the animals on these two pages are endangered.

While governments are working to protect species and their habitats, it's estimated that more species are threatened with extinction every day. For people who appreciate the beauty and strength of animals and would like to see them remain safely and happily in the wild, it's important to take steps to save the environment.

Mountain gorilla, Rwanda

American crocodile, United States

One easy thing you can do to help save animals is to recycle things like cans, bottles and paper, so there's less garbage on earth and more room for forest, field, stream, jungle, and ocean . . . and more room for the animals who share our world.

Black rhinoceros, Kenya The black rhino is one of the most severely endangered large mammals in the world. Nearly extinct in Asia, the last of this species lives on the open grasslands of Kenya, where the government has to work hard to guard the rhinoceros from hunters.

Snow leopard, China

Thick-billed parrot, United States This is the only surviving parrot native to the United States. Only a few of the birds survive in their natural habitat in the Chihuahua Mountains of Arizona.

31

Glossary

civilization a complex society with a stable food supply, division of labor, some form of government, and a highly developed culture (p. 24)

climate the average weather conditions of a region over a period of years (p. 19)

culture the beliefs and customs of a group of people that are passed on from generation to generation (p. 13)

deity a god or spiritual power (p. 8)

depose to remove from office (p. 12)

domesticate to tame (p. 8)

ecosystem how the plants, animals, earth, air, water, and energy in an area (such as a forest or desert) interact with one another to create a specific kind of environment (p. 30)

emblem symbol; something that stands for an idea, belief, or nation (p. 12)

environment natural surroundings (p. 9)

evacuate to move people away from a place quickly, often because of an emergency (p. 7)

habitat a place where an animal or plant normally lives (p. 5)

instincts natural tendencies or impulses that cause animals to act in characteristic ways (p. 6)

larva an insect in its early stage as a caterpillar, grub, or maggot, between hatching from an egg and becoming a pupa (p. 19)

mallet a long-handled wooden hammer used in polo and croquet (p. 28)

mythical legendary (p. 17)

native born, grown, or originating in a particular place or country (p. 4)

nomadic referring to people who move from place to place (p. 19)

prehistoric occurring before the time when humans began recording history through writing (p. 6)

prominence importance (p. 13)

prophet a person who foretells the future or a person who speaks or writes as with a message from God (p. 14)

protein a nutrient that is a necessary part of the human diet; it is found especially in meat, milk, nuts, and eggs (p. 19)

recycle to use over again (p. 30)

remote isolated, far away (p. 6)

sacred holy (p. 8)

scarce not plentiful; hard to find (p. 25)

shepherd a person who watches over and guides a herd of animals (p. 26)

signifies stands for, symbolizes (p. 12)

social status the position or rank of a person in relation to others in his or her society (p. 12)

spiritual religious (p. 14)

superstition the belief that supernatural forces exist and that certain actions will either please or anger them, causing either good or bad things to happen (p. 14)

Index

Alaska, 10, 23, 24
Algeria, 7
alpacas, 20, 21
animal rights, 18
Argentina, 9
armadillos, 9
Assyrians, 6
Australia, 4, 19
bears, 5, 15, 20, 28
Bedouins, 22
beliefs and animals, 14-17
birds, 6, 7, 8, 9, 10, 12, 19, 31
Bolivia, 13
Brazil, 10
camels, 18, 19, 22, 24
Canada, 10, 11, 12, 24, 28
carrier pigeons, 26
cats, 4, 8, 14
cattle, 13, 14, 18, 19, 21, 26
chameleons, 10, 11
China, 6, 20, 23, 31
circuses, 28
dogs, 4, 8, 10, 11, 12, 24, 26, 27
Ecuador, 13
Egypt, 8, 14, 24
elephants, 7, 25, 28
endangered animals, 30-31
England, 14, 17, 28
fish, 15, 16, 18, 19
France, 12
goats, 18, 20
Greece, 16, 17
Guatemala, 12
guinea pigs, 8
Hawaii, 6
hippopotami, 5
Hong Kong, 17
Hopi people, 15
horses, 6, 7, 16, 24, 25
Iceland, 19
iguanas, 8
India, 7, 14, 16, 22
Indonesia, 19, 28
Inuit people, 20
Japan, 15, 20
Jordan, 22
Kazakhstan, 23
Kenya, 13, 18, 31
lions, 28
llamas, 13, 18, 20
Madagascar, 4, 10, 11
Malaysia, 24
Mexico, 5, 9
monkeys, 10, 14, 15, 26
Morocco, 9
mules, 24
mythical creatures, 16-17
Nepal, 24
New Zealand, 21
Nigeria, 14
Norway, 12
Paraguay, 25
Peru, 13
pets, 8-11
Poland, 4
rabbits, 4
rats, 7, 14
reindeer, 12, 25
rhinoceros, 31
Rwanda, 30
Scotland, 26
seals, 20
sheep, 20, 21
Siberia, 25
silk, 20
Singapore, 5
snow leopard, 31
Tahiti, 6
Tanzania, 13, 23
tarantulas, 11
Thailand, 25, 26
three-toed sloth, 10
tigers, 28
traveling by animal, 24-25
unicorns, 16
United Arab Emirates, 13
water buffalo, 24
wool, 20, 21
work and animals, 26-27
yaks, 24
Yemen, 21
Zimbabwe, 5, 27
zoos, 4

About the Author

Sara Corbett is a writer who lives in Santa Fe, New Mexico, with a dog named Trout and a cat named Flash. This book is dedicated to her mother, who allowed her to have gerbils, turtles, rabbits, and chameleons as pets when she was young.